The Secret Language of Men

by Sherrie Weaver

0 43422 69541 6

During the course of my marriage and raising a son, I have learned many things. I have learned to be very careful when changing a boy's diaper, never to use the bathroom in the middle of the night without checking the seat position, and that reminding husbands of impending birthdays and anniversaries will avoid big fights.

But the most important lesson of all is the hardest one to learn: Men do not always say what they mean. Of course, neither do women, but a book about the secret language of women would have been only one page. That page would read: *If you really loved me, you'd know exactly what I meant.*

So in the interest of better communication, and promoting mutual understanding between men and women, I'm offering the following interpretations. It comes highly recommended by my husband, who said he would be glad to read it, *except he's very busy.*

S.W.

"I can't talk right now."

"Me and the guys in the sales department are photocopying the receptionist."

"I'm really busy."

"Baywatch is on, and it's the one where they lose their swimsuits in the undertow."

"I'm going fishing."

"I'm going to drink myself dangerously stupid, and stand by a stream with a stick in my hand, while the fish swim by in complete safety."

"I don't care where we eat."

"Whatever restaurant you choose will be wrong, but I won't say anything until we're halfway through the meal."

"No, don't dress up, this is supposed to be a casual deal."

"Wear a formal gown with gloves and high heels."

"Let's take your car."

"Mine is full of beer cans, burger wrappers and completely out of gas."

"No, my new secretary isn't pretty."

*"She was 'Miss December'
two years in a row."*

"Honey, you know a woman's bustline isn't important to me."

"A woman with huge mammary glands will cause my entire neurological system to shut down, and I will drool incessantly."

"Woman driver."

"Someone who doesn't speed, tailgate, swear, make obscene gestures and has a better driving record than me."

"I don't care what color you paint the kitchen."

"As long as it's not blue, green, pink, red, yellow, lavender, gray, mauve, black, turquoise or any other color besides white."

SCIENTIFIC RESEARCH SHOWS:

When a husband and wife argue, the husband will usually blame the wife's hormonal cycle.

2 out of every 4 men have no idea what to do with a sponge mop.

"Are you still on the phone?"

"I have a new joke based on a sexual premise which would offend a semi-sentient bacterial culture and I want to tell it to my friends, who will probably choke on their cornchips laughing."

15

"He's henpecked."

"Once, in a moment of extreme weakness, he made a decision based remotely on something his wife said."

"It's a guy thing."

"There is no rational thought pattern connected with it, and you have no chance at all of making it logical."

17

"Can I help with dinner?"

"Why isn't it already on the table?"

18

"Uh huh," "Sure, honey," or "Yes, dear."

Absolutely nothing. It's a conditioned response like Pavlov's dog drooling.

19

"Good idea."

"It'll never work. And I'll spend the rest of the day gloating."

20

"Have you lost weight?"

"I've just spent our last $30 on a cordless drill."

"I could never date anyone else."

"Because you'd catch me."

"I'll fix dinner."

"No more tuna surprise,
I've reached my limit."

23

"We make a good couple."

"You own a boat, fishing rods, and can bait your own hook."

24

SCIENTIFIC RESEARCH SHOWS:

Most men believe that the four food groups are beer, chips, ice cream and pizza.

82% of all males experience symptoms of anxiety if they hear the word *commitment.*

"I'm sorry, it was my fault."

"I've got to get some sleep, and need to bring this argument to a hasty close."

"My wife doesn't understand me."

"She's heard all my stories before, and is tired of them."

27 ♂

"I'll always love you."

"As long as you're young, thin, and don't make me watch the 'Sound of Music' on TV."

28

"No, I don't mind if your mother visits us for a while."

"I'm going camping for an entire month."

"That's a new look for you, isn't it?"

"You look ridiculous."

30

"You spend too much money."

"There is not enough left in our savings to buy my new truck."

"Whatever you want is fine."

"Go away and leave me alone."

32

"It would take too long to explain."

"I have no idea how it works."

33

"Boy's night out."

"Liquor, stupid, tasteless jokes, and pastrami sandwiches in a sports bar."

"I've got a special evening planned."

"The Monster truck tractor pulls and a whole bag of pork rinds."

♂ 35

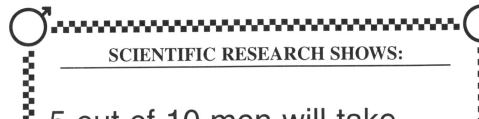

SCIENTIFIC RESEARCH SHOWS:

5 out of 10 men will take reading material into the toilet with them.

Of those, 4 are not even remotely embarrassed.

"I'm getting more exercise lately."

"The batteries in the remote are dead."

"When are you planning on getting groceries?"

"We're out of chips and salsa."

"Give me a chance to unwind before you start nagging."

"In 15 minutes, I'll be asleep on the sofa and won't hear a thing you say."

"Some of the guys are coming over to watch the game."

"There will soon be a group of mouth-breathing primates trashing our living room and slapping each other on the back."

"Rough day at the office."

"We were out of coffee creamer, and we had to wait 30 minutes to tee off."

"I got a lot done."

"I found 'Waldo' in almost every picture."

"We're going to be late."

"Now I have a legitimate excuse to drive like a maniac."

"Is this that P.M.S. thing I've been hearing about."

"Please put the axe down and back away slowly."

"Hey, I've read all the classics ."

"I've been subscribing to Playboy since 1972."

"You cook just like my mother used to."

"She used the smoke detector as a meal timer, too."

SCIENTIFIC RESEARCH SHOWS:

72% of all male football fans believe that Superbowl Sunday is a national holiday.

Most men would prefer to pave the lawn than deal with yardwork.

"I'm very supportive of you."

"I'll hold the ladder while you paint the ceiling."

"I was listening to you. It's just that I have things on my mind."

"I was wondering whether that red-head over there is wearing a bra."

"I'll mow the lawn."

"The neighbor's teenaged cheerleader daughters are sunbathing."

"Take a break, honey, you're working too hard."

"I can't hear the game over the vacuum cleaner."

"That's interesting, dear."

"Are you still talking?"

52

"That's a nice dress."

"How much did it cost?"

53

"Honey, we don't need material things to prove our love."

"I forgot our anniversary again."

"You're the perfect woman for me."

"No one else would put up with me."

55

"You need some companionship around here."

"I just bought a Great Dane."

"I was being over-managed in that job."

"How was I supposed to know she was the bosses' daughter?"

SCIENTIFIC RESEARCH SHOWS:

For every 1 diaper a new dad changes, a new mom changes 13.

The average bachelor cooks a meal 3 times a week, and believes it is balanced if it consists of nachos and beer.

"She's a pushy witch."

"She's an aggressive working woman."

"You expect too much of me."

"You want me to stay awake."

"It's a really good movie."

"It's got guns, knives, fast cars, and Heather Locklear."

61 ♂

"That's women's work."

"It's difficult, dirty, and thankless."

62

"Honey, I love you. Let's renew our wedding vows, buy you a bigger diamond and take a cruise."

"I've just slept with your sister."

63

"Will you marry me?"

"Both my roommates have moved out, I can't find the washer, and there is no more peanut butter."

64

"I am not having a mid-life crisis."

"I think all paunchy, middle-aged, balding men should grow a pony tail and buy in-line skates."

65

"She meant nothing to me."

"Of course, neither do you."

"I just need my own space."

"My new secretary is a full 38C and single."

67

"They don't make them like this anymore."

"Replacement parts will be scarce, backordered, and very expensive."

"Go ask your mother."

"I am incapable of making a decision."

"I've got some important things to do today."

"I would rather be boiled in molten lead than to go shopping with you."

"You know how bad my memory is."

"I remember the theme song to 'F Troop,' the address of the first girl I ever kissed and the Vehicle Identification Numbers of every car I've owned, but I forgot your birthday."

"I never know what to buy you for Christmas."

"The thought of entering a department store freezes my blood."

"Flowers are so, I don't know, trivial and common."

"What, you can have them delivered nowadays? Since when?"

"I was just thinking about you, and got you these roses."

"The girl selling them on the corner was a real babe."

"No, that dress doesn't make you look fat."

"That extra 30 pounds of grease on your behind, now that makes you look fat."

"Football is a man's game."

"Women are generally too smart to play it."

"Okay, okay, we'll talk."

"You'll yell, I'll ignore you."

SCIENTIFIC RESEARCH SHOWS:

95% of men over age 35 think that the picture of dogs playing poker qualifies as fine art.

Every 15 minutes, somewhere in the world, a man falls asleep on his sofa.

"Oh, don't fuss. I just cut myself, it's no big deal."

"I have actually severed a limb, but will bleed to death before I admit I'm hurt."

79

"I do help around the house."

"I once put a dirty towel in the laundry basket."

"I'll be out of the office all day."

"I've got an all day pass to the Sportsmen's Show."

"Hey, I've got my reasons for what I'm doing."

"And I sure hope I think of some pretty soon."

82

"I'll be glad to take the garbage out."

"Please take that knife out of my ribs."

83

"Do you think my hair is getting thin?"

"Has my forehead always gone back behind my ears?"

84 ♂

"I can't find it?"

"It didn't fall into my outstretched hands, so I'm completely clueless."

"Is it that time, is that why you're so cranky?"

"I'd like to sleep on the couch for the rest of my adult life."

"I can't talk to you when you're like this."

"When you're being logical, I can't bury you in so much verbal manure."

87

"Ah, it's just a head cold, I'll be all right."

"After you've waited on me hand and foot for two days."

88

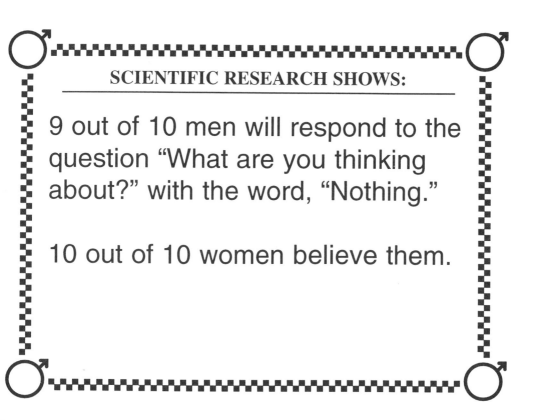

SCIENTIFIC RESEARCH SHOWS:

9 out of 10 men will respond to the question "What are you thinking about?" with the word, "Nothing."

10 out of 10 women believe them.

"A man's gotta do what a man's gotta do."

"And a woman's gotta clean up after him."

"What did I do this time?"

"What did you catch me at?"

"What do you mean, you need new clothes?"

"You just bought new clothes 3 years ago."

"Want to go to a movie?"

"The air conditioning in my apartment is out."

"You're too emotional."

"I had my feelings surgically removed when I was 12."

94

"Isn't that just like a woman?"

"Logical, efficient, and effective."

95

"She's one of those rabid feminists."

"She refused to make my coffee."

96

"But I hate to go shopping."

"Because I always wind up outside the dressing room holding your purse."

97

"Trust me, it won't rain."

"Pack wet weather gear, an umbrella, and an ark."

"No, I left plenty of gas in the car."

"You may actually get it to start."

99

SCIENTIFIC RESEARCH SHOWS:

The average male spends 4 hours a day thinking about the female anatomy.

6 out of 10 men can belch and make it sound like a swear word.

"I'm still in the same physical shape as when I was 16."

"I couldn't do 10 push-ups then, either."

"I'm listening to you."

*"Every once in a while,
a word or two makes it
through the newspaper and TV."*

"Do you think money grows on trees?"

"I need a chrome roll bar for the truck, so groceries can wait."

"I'm not the romantic type."

*"Once you catch the bus,
you stop running."*

"Stop trying to change me."

"I haven't brushed my teeth in 12 years, and see no reason to start now."

"You're just spending money on frivolous things."

"Do you really need to buy braces for the kids, car insurance and toilet paper?"

"I'm taking the kids to the park."

"You're so grouchy, I'd do anything to get out of here."

"I don't want to argue with you."

"You have a valid point, and I can't refute it."

"Sure, I'll help you pick up."

"I have no intentions of moving from this chair until this place is classified as a Superfund site, and is in imminent danger of spontaneously combusting."

"I'm going to stop off for a quick one with the guys."

"I am planning on drinking myself into a vegetative state with my chest pounding, mouth breathing, pre-evolutionary companions."

SCIENTIFIC RESEARCH SHOWS:

6 out of 10 men cannot locate the dirty clothes hamper in their homes.

10 out of 10 men are able to find the TV remote control, even blindfolded.

"I heard you."

"I haven't the foggiest clue what you just said, and am hoping desperately that I can fake it well enough so that you don't spend the next three days yelling at me."

112

"You know I could never love anyone else."

"I am used to the way you yell at me, and realize it could be worse."

"I was not looking at that girl."

"It is highly likely that I will have to wear a neck brace for a while, because I dislocated several vertebrae whirling my head around to stare at her legs."

114 ♂

"I want to be with you tonight."

"I am out of chips and beer, and there is nothing on TV."

115

"You look terrific."

"Oh, God, please don't try on one more outfit. I'm starving."

"What's for dinner?"

"Please tell me we're finally out of that tuna noodle thing your mother brought over last week."

"Don't call a repairman, I can fix that."

"I'll spend all weekend swearing at inanimate objects, throwing tools at the cat and cursing like a drunken sailor, so you can call the repairman Monday."

118

"I'll mow the lawn right after the game."

"After the Superbowl, which is in January. The lawn will be under 4 feet of snow, and will no longer need mowing."

119

"I brought you a present."

"It was free ice scraper night at the ball game."

120

"I'm going to watch the game."

"I am going to lock myself in the den with a 12 pack and a bag of Doritos. The next time you lay eyes on me, I will be living proof that Adam was a rough draft."

121

SCIENTIFIC RESEARCH SHOWS:

17 minutes is the longest amount of time a man can go without thinking about a car or truck.

14 out of 20 men will automatically take the armrest on an airline seat.

"Let's watch some TV."

"I'll punch buttons on the remote control until you are tempted to ram it deeply into my left ear. Then you will become extremely frustrated with me and go away."

123

"Man, what a long day."

"Leave me alone, and let me sleep on the couch until midnight."

124

" I missed you."

"I can't find my sock drawer, the kids are hungry and we are out of toilet paper."

125

"I'm not lost.
I know exactly where we are."

"No one will ever see us alive again."

126

"Okay. if it's that important to you, we can talk about our relationship."

"Like dental work, I must undergo this painful process every year."

127

"We share the household chores."

*"I make the messes,
she cleans them up."*

128

"I'm going to work on the car for a while."

"If I have to sit through one more black and white romance movie, I'll go completely mad."

129

"People change."

"My old girlfriend just won the lottery."

"It's just not working out. I think we should break up."

"I no longer have time to spend on my friends, my car, and my dog."

131 ♂

"This relationship is getting too serious."

"I like you more than my truck."

132

95% of men think that belching is a sign of virility.

After 8 years of marriage, men do not see a reason for sexy lingerie.

"Of course I like it, honey, you look beautiful."

"Oh, man, what have you done to yourself?"

"We should spend more time together."

"Come out to the garage and help me change the oil in the car."

"I need a change of scenery."

"I'd like to look at other women for a while."

"I recycle."

"We could pay the rent with the money from my empties."

"His wife doesn't work."

"She has three kids, a huge house, and her husband spends all his time with his mistress."

"My ex-wife really took me to the cleaners."

"I have to pay child support."

"Hunting season is almost here."

"Pretty soon, my hunter/gatherer buddies and I will spend one week in a mountain tent, passing gas and handling firearms."

"My wife is a good cook."

"I never have to eat microwave burritos."

"I enjoy sports."

"We have a big screen TV and all 500 cable channels."

"I hate the holidays."

"If she drags me to the 'Nutcracker' again this year, I'm going to kill her."

SCIENTIFIC RESEARCH SHOWS:

96% of all married men believe not passing gas in bed constitutes foreplay.

No man can stay awake longer than 18 minutes after Thanksgiving dinner.

"I'm a homeowner."

"Now I have a whole lot of chores to ignore."

"We should go to Hawaii for our vacation."

"I want to see the new thong bikinis."

146

"Let's spend the night together."

*"I don't want to go home.
My apartment is a mess."*

"Do I have to dress up?"

*"I want to wear jeans,
a faded t-shirt, and no tie."*

148

"I was entertaining a client."

"All the money I lost at the track last night is tax deductable."

"It sure snowed last night."

"I suppose you're going to nag me about shoveling the walk now."

"It's good beer."

"It was on sale."

"I don't need to read the instructions."

"I am perfectly capable of screwing it up without printed help."

"The grunge look is in."

"I have neither showered nor shaved in 4 days."

153

"I'm making a fashion statement."

"I'm wearing thermal underwear and a sweatband."

SCIENTIFIC RESEARCH SHOWS:

If a female begins a sentence with "Honey, would you...," 87% of males go instantly deaf.

19 out of 20 times, if either member of an engaged couple is having serious second thoughts, it will be the male.

"I'll fix the garbage disposal later."

"If I wait long enough you'll get frustrated and buy a new one."

"I'm going on a business trip."

"Three days in Southern California, all expenses paid, and there is nothing you can do about it."

157

"What's wrong with my driving?"

"Don't you want to be a part of the Indy 500?"

158

"Honey, you should go visit your family this weekend."

"The playoffs are on, which means 36 uninterrupted hours of vegetative TV watching."

159

"I'm going to be spending a lot more time with my family."

"I've been fired."

160

"We can't afford a vacation this year."

"I would have to be heavily sedated to get in a car with you and those kids again."

161

"I don't need a map, I can find this place, no problem."

"I'll drive around in a circle for 30 minutes, growing increasingly more irritable until you finally force me, at gunpoint, to ask for directions."

"I'll take you to a fancy restaurant."

"Some place that doesn't have a drive through window."

163

"I broke up with her."

"She dumped me."

164

"She dumped me for no reason."

"I stood her up one too many times, and now she won't accept the charges when I call her collect."

165

"I consider myself a man of the world."

"I owe money in 14 different countries."

SCIENTIFIC RESEARCH SHOWS:

72% of all men surveyed said they would marry again, if they had to do it over.

86% of the women asked were laughing too hard to answer!

Other Titles By Great Quotations

201 Best Things Ever Said
The ABC's of Parenting
As a Cat Thinketh
The Best of Friends
The Birthday Astrologer
Chicken Soup & Other Yiddish Say
Cornerstones of Success
Don't Deliberate ... Litigate!
Fantastic Father, Dependable Dad
Global Wisdom
Golden Years, Golden Words
Grandma, I Love You
Growing up in Toyland
Happiness is Found Along The Way
Hollywords
Hooked on Golf
In Celebration of Women
Inspirations Compelling Food for Thought
I'm Not Over the Hill
Let's Talk Decorating
Life's Lessons
Life's Simple Pleasures
A Light Heart Lives Long
Money for Nothing, Tips for Free

Mother, I Love You
Motivating Quotes for Motivated People
Mrs. Aesop's Fables
Mrs. Murphy's Laws
Mrs. Webster's Dictionary
My Daughter, My Special Friend
Other Species
Parenting 101
Reflections
Romantic Rhapsody
The Secret Language of Men
The Secret Language of Women
Some Things Never Change
The Sports Page
Sports Widow
Stress or Sanity
Teacher is Better than Two Books
Teenage of Insanity
Thanks from the Heart
Things You'll Learn if You Live Long Enough
Wedding Wonders
Working Women's World
Interior Design for Idiots
Dear Mr. President

GREAT QUOTATIONS PUBLISHING COMPANY
1967 Quincy Court
Glendale Heights, IL 60139 - 2045
Phone (630) 582-2800
Fax (630) 582- 2813